EXODUS

Brian Wildsmith

Oxford University Press

Oxford Toronto Melbourne

YOU MUST HONOUR YOUR
            FATHER AND MOTHER.
YOU MUST NOT KILL.
YOU MUST NOT TAKE SOMEONE
            ELSE'S HUSBAND OR WIFE.
YOU MUST NOT STEAL.
YOU MUST NOT ACCUSE ANYONE UNJUSTLY.
YOU MUST NOT COVET THINGS
            THAT BELONG TO OTHER PEOPLE.

For Clare, Rebecca, Anna, and Simon

Oxford University Press, Great Clarendon Street, Oxford OX2 6DP

Oxford New York
Athens Auckland Bangkok Bogota Buenos Aires Calcutta
Cape Town Chennai Dar es Salaam Delhi Florence Hong Kong Istanbul
Karachi Kuala Lumpur Madrid Melbourne Mexico City Mumbai
Nairobi Paris Sao Paulo Singapore Taipei Tokyo Toronto Warsaw

and associated companies in
Berlin Ibadan

Oxford is a trade mark of Oxford University Press

British Library Cataloguing in Publication Data
Data available

ISBN 0 19 279025 0

Typeset in Plantin
by Mike Brain

Printed in Hong Kong

WHEN the Hebrews were slaves in Egypt, a Hebrew woman gave birth to a son. Now Pharaoh had ordered that all the Hebrew baby boys should be killed. The mother made a basket of bullrushes, placed her baby inside, and hid it among the reeds. Her daughter Miriam kept watch.

Some time later Pharaoh's daughter came down to the river to bathe. She heard the baby crying and picked him up. She felt sorry for the little boy.

Miriam came forward and asked, 'Shall I go and find one of the Hebrew women to nurse the child for you?'

So Miriam fetched the baby's mother. Pharaoh's daughter said, 'Look after this little boy for me and I will pay you.'

The woman took the baby and nursed him, and when he was old enough she brought him back to Pharaoh's daughter. She named him Moses.

MOSES grew up as an Egyptian prince, surrounded by the riches of Egypt. But he never forgot that he was a Hebrew and he hated the cruel way his people were treated.

One day he saw an Egyptian guard whipping a Hebrew slave. Moses was so angry that he leapt at the guard and killed him with his bare hands.

WHEN Pharoah heard of this, he was very angry. He summoned the captain of the guard and ordered him to arrest Moses.

But Moses fled to the land of Midian where he lived and worked as a shepherd for many years.

In time Pharaoh died and was replaced by another king. He was just as cruel, and the Hebrews in Egypt suffered even more.

ONE day Moses was looking after his flock when God appeared to him as a fire blazing out from a bush. But although the bush was on fire, it was not burnt up.

God called to Moses from out of the flames: 'Take off your shoes for you are standing on holy ground. I am your God and I have seen the suffering of my people. Go back to Egypt, and tell Pharaoh to let my people go. You will lead them out of Egypt to a land flowing with milk and honey.'

Then God spoke to Moses's brother, Aaron, in Egypt. 'Your brother is coming home. Go and meet him.'

THE two brothers met and they went to Pharaoh's court together. They said: 'The Lord God has sent us to tell you to set his people free and let them go.'

'I do not know your God,' replied Pharaoh. 'Show me a sign from him.'

Aaron threw his staff to the ground and it turned into a snake. When Pharaoh called his magicians to throw down their staffs, they became snakes too. But Aaron's snake swallowed up all their snakes.

Pharaoh took no notice. 'No,' he said. 'I will not let you go.'

SO God sent a series of plagues to strike Egypt. The Nile turned to blood, and Egypt was invaded by frogs, insects, and flies. The cattle died, people were covered in boils, there were fierce hailstorms, locusts ate up all the corn, and there was darkness for three days. Still Pharaoh would not let the Hebrews go.

Finally God said to Moses: 'Tonight all the eldest sons in the land will die, but you will be safe if you do as I command.' And so each Hebrew family killed a lamb and painted its blood on their doorposts.

They roasted the lamb and ate it with flat loaves and bitter herbs and waited while the angel of death passed over them. Hebrews still remember this time and celebrate it with a feast called Passover.

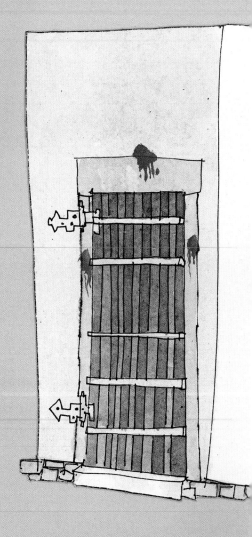

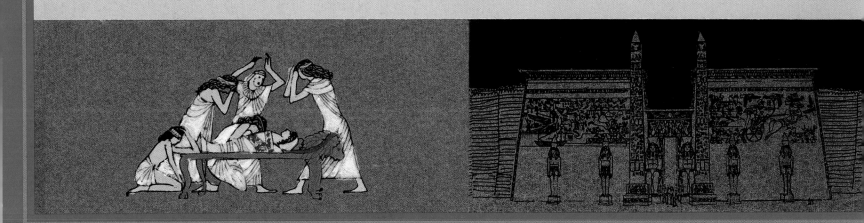

A great cry rose up in Egypt, a cry of grief for the dead sons. Pharaoh summoned Moses and Aaron to him. 'Leave this land! Leave, or we shall all be dead!'

The Hebrews left Egypt that night, six hundred thousand people,
together with their flocks and cattle. Moses led the way, and by his
side was a young boy named Joshua.

G OD led the way in a pillar of cloud by day, and a pillar of flames to guide them during the night.

BUT Pharaoh changed his mind and sent his chariots after them. When the Egyptians caught up with them, the Hebrews had reached the Red Sea. But God caused the pillar of cloud to bring darkness on the Egyptians and the pillar of flame to bring light to the Hebrews. So the two armies were kept apart.

Then God sent a powerful east wind, which parted the waters in two.
The Hebrews walked through the middle of the sea on dry ground
and crossed safely to the other side. When the Egyptians tried to
follow, the sea came roaring down on them and swept them away.

THE Hebrews travelled on into the wilderness. After three days the food
ran out and the people complained bitterly that they were hungry.
Next day, in the early morning, God covered the ground with food for them.

It was white, tasted of honey, and Moses called it manna. All the time they were in the desert God gave them manna to eat.

G OD also sent them flocks of birds called quails, which they cooked and ate.

THE Hebrews went deeper into
the desert. The sun beat down on
them and there was no water. They began
to quarrel with Moses. 'We should have stayed
in Egypt,' they cried. 'We will all die of thirst here.'

God told Moses to strike a rock with his staff. Suddenly fresh water gushed
out and they all had enough to drink.

AFTER three month's travelling the Hebrews came to the foot of Mount Sinai. God called out to Moses to meet him, so Moses went up to the top of the mountain amidst thunder and lightning, flames of fire, and the blast of trumpets. There God gave him Ten Commandments, written on two tablets of stone. These were the laws which told the people how they should live.

MOSES stayed on the mountain for so long that the people grew angry and impatient. They shouted at Aaron: 'What has happened to Moses? Where is his God now? Make us another god, a god that we can see.' So Aaron collected their golden jewellery, melted it down, and made them a golden calf.

When Moses returned, the people were dancing and
worshipping the calf of gold. Moses was so angry that he broke
the tablets God had given him and destroyed the golden calf.

BUT God forgave his people and ordered Moses to cut two new tablets of stone. Moses carried them up the mountain and God wrote out his commandments again.

When Moses came down, his face was shining because he had been talking with God. And all the people listened as Moses taught them the laws of God.

FOR forty years the Hebrews travelled through the wilderness until at last they reached the edge of the Jordan valley. From the top of a high mountain God showed Moses the beautiful land of Canaan. 'This is the land I promised to give my people,' He said. 'I have let you see it at a distance but you shall not enter it.'

And there Moses died. His people buried him in a peaceful valley, and they wept for him for thirty days.

THEN Joshua, who had first followed Moses when he was a boy, took his place and led the Hebrews into the promised land.

After all their wanderings and struggles, they were a free people at last.
They had finally come home.

THE TEN COMMANDMENTS

I AM YOUR GOD.
I rescued you from Egypt
where you lived as slaves.
YOU MUST NOT WORSHIP ANY OTHER GODS.
YOU MUST NOT MAKE ANY IDOLS
OR IMAGES TO WORSHIP.
YOU MUST NOT USE MY NAME WRONGFULLY.
YOU MUST DO NO WORK ON
THE SABBATH DAY.